DENCH.

DENCH.

recipes and stories from
the college pop-up

Jimmy Wong

photography by Carly Lamera

Jimmy Wong
San Luis Obispo, CA

www.denchrestaurant.com
@jwongdynasty

FIRST EDITION

Cover by Carly Lamera
Design and Photography by Carly Lamera
Photo Editing by Monica Andres, Jessica Dong, Michelle Kang, Carly Lamera

Printed in Canada.

ISBN 978-0-578-49108-0

To Uncle Craig

A special thanks to…

Mom & Dad,

Janette & Jennie,

Derrick, Zachary, Jeremiah, & Lucas,

Jeffrey & Sharon Armstrong,

Luke & Jane Faber,

Peter & Leslie Orradre,

Danny & Estella Wong,

& all of the supporters who made this book possible.

TABLE OF CONTENTS

INTRODUCTION   1

COURSE ONE   Canapé   14

COURSE TWO   Bread   22

COURSE THREE   Pre-Entrée   28

COURSE FOUR   Main Course   38

COURSE FIVE   Intermezzo   48

COURSE SIX   Dessert   54

COURSE SEVEN   Mignardise   78

ADDITIONAL RECIPES   92

TIMELINE AND LAYOUT   94

INTRODUCTION

RUNNING A RESTAURANT was always a dream of mine…Who would've thought my first hustle would be out of my college studio apartment.

DENCH. is the pop-up restaurant I opened in San Luis Obispo, California at the beginning of my junior year in college in 2017. At DENCH., I offered a seven-course tasting menu for four people once a week, all out of my tiny studio apartment. The dishes I served at the pop-up were a reflection of who I am and featured some of San Luis Obispo's finest seasonal ingredients. I served as DENCH.'s only cook, host, server, busser, dishwasher, and PR agent.

The pop-up restaurant was operated out of my studio which I converted to be essentially 70% kitchen space. The only thing that separated me, the kitchen, and the guests was a stainless steel prep table where everyone was able to watch me as I plated and cooked their meal. It was kind of like an open kitchen restaurant…if real restaurants had their guests sit a couple feet away from the chef's bed.

I thought doing the pop-up was the best path for me to learn about myself as a cook and the food I would want to put out in my future restaurant. I figured this was the way I could express myself creatively on my own terms. Guests could give me their instant feedback of what they enjoyed or didn't enjoy about the food or ambiance which allowed me to fine-tune the whole DENCH. experience.

This book includes the recipes to all 28 different dishes and items I served over the year doing the pop-up. While the menu wouldn't change week to week, dishes would come and go based on seasonality and availability.

If you're wondering why the pop-up is called DENCH., the story is probably not as profound as you might think. Back in high school, my friends and I used to follow this one soccer player from England named Emmanuel Frimpong. I guess he really liked the actress Dame Judi Dench because he used to say things like, "that's dench, bruv", as a way to say something was "cool" or "sick". The phrase "dench" kind of stuck with us and we started to do things like sneak it into our essays to see if our teachers would notice. I started hashtagging all of my pictures on Instagram #dench and if you click on it, you'll mainly just see buff British men and sometimes my food. When it came time to name the pop-up, only one name really made sense.

CUPERTINO, CALIFORNIA

GROWING UP AS THE YOUNGEST in a family of five under Chinese immigrant parents in the South Bay, I would always try to find ways to get away from my culture in order to assimilate into the American culture that surrounded me. I would avoid things like my mom's whole steamed fish or stir-fried veggies in the pursuit of the exotic American delicacies I saw my friends eating at school. Man, Hot Pockets and Lunchables never looked so good.

Deep down, I think I always knew I loved my mom's cooking. My admiration for her cooking is probably what led me to my interest in food. (Mom, you can blame your signature roast pork for why I'm into cooking and not doctoring like you hoped). For some reason, I was always drawn to the pastry side of the kitchen and my first foray into cooking was decorating cupcakes in middle school. I got my first job in a restaurant at sixteen as a busser in a local Japanese restaurant that my English teacher used to be a sushi chef at. I went into the job wanting to learn more about the restaurant industry and I worked my way up the front-of-house, going from bussing tables to hosting, then finally serving. But it wasn't enough to me—I wanted to learn more about working back-of-house and I didn't think the scary Vietnamese cooks at this establishment were the teachers I was really looking for.

I didn't know too much about the restaurant scene in my area at the time so I went on Yelp and looked up every four-dollar sign place within a ten mile radius from my house. I then wrote an email to each of them asking if I could come kick it with them over the summer. To my surprise, the only restaurants that got back to me were the ones with Michelin stars. So, at seventeen, I spent my summer staging, or apprenticing, under the pastry chefs at two different Michelin-starred restaurants. I would spend two days at Plumed Horse in Saratoga, two days at Chez TJ in Mountain View, and one day serving tables at the Japanese restaurant, Kiku Sushi. It was in these kitchens that I really solidified my passion for cooking at a higher level. The pressure, precision, and perfection of it all appealed to me like nothing else had before. Outside the time spent helping prep for dinner service, plating dishes for guests, and pissing my chefs off for being slow, I began to see how all the chefs would rely on their experiences and cultural backgrounds to create their own unique and personal dishes. Slowly, I realized how important my upbringing was in how I wanted to express myself as a cook.

When time came around to decide what I wanted to do after high school, I had to choose between culinary school and college. As you might have figured, I ended up going college at the California Polytechnic State University, San Luis Obispo for a degree in food science. I figured that if I could learn about food on a chemical, biological, and microbiological level, and combine that with culinary skills, I could make some pretty cool dishes.

CREATING DENCH.

IF IT WEREN'T FOR A LONG LIST of different situations and experiences that perfectly lined up, the pop-up never would have existed. During my sophomore year in college, I struggled a lot with finding purpose at Cal Poly. I didn't feel as though I had a community, friends, or more importantly, a reason for being in SLO. I looked around at all of the different chefs I looked up to and saw that so few of them had college degrees, and even if they did, practically none of them had anything to do with food. It was like I was wasting my time in school learning about how to process a can of string beans when I could've been out in the world working to become like the chefs I aspired to be. I just really didn't feel like there was anything for me in SLO.

After a lot of time contemplating things…I called my parents to tell them that I was going to drop out of college in the fall of 2016. That, for me, was the hardest conversation that I've ever had. My nineteen-year-old brain convinced me that it was something I just had to do yet I knew how much I was disappointing my parents. I could see how hurt they were and how it was making them question themselves if it was something they did wrong for me to feel this way. Even after hanging up the phone, I still felt like dropping out was the right thing for me to do.

I spent some more time thinking about the decision and figured I should call my old pastry chef from Chez TJ to get her advice. We had spent hours talking to each other while working together about my plans after high school and what to expect from the restaurant industry. She was also one of the very few people I met who even had a college degree before going into the industry. I hadn't spoken to her since high school so I texted her to set up a time for a call. Over that two-hour call, I realized that she was probably the only person I could have contacted that could have empathized with what I was going through and provide me with the advice I needed to hear. While I was considering dropping my degree in food science to go into the restaurant industry, she had just left the restaurant industry to pursue a degree in food science. She told me that college was the best place for me to be at the moment. I was scared that I was going to be too old to start cooking professionally by the time I graduated, but she assured me that I would still be young and spritely at twenty-two and ready to work in any restaurant. She continued by saying that the time I spend in college would only make me hungrier to pursue my passion for cooking in restaurants—if that's truly what I wanted. I took what she said to heart and my decision to drop out began to shift. The more I thought about it, the more I was convinced that the conversation I had with my pastry chef was too perfect to simply be a coincidence or luck.

I took the next couple weeks to continue to think over my decision and pray about things. It was during this time that I really heard God telling me that there were more things and people He had in store for me in SLO. There was a reason He brought me to Cal Poly and I hadn't yet figured out why. I wasn't sure what He had in store for my future and if it was even going to be enjoyable or fulfilling, but I trusted that it was going to be what was best for me and made my final decision to stay in school.

I always wanted to do pop-up dinners in college ever since high school when I saw kids online running restaurants out of their dorms. I had just signed a lease for a studio apartment, freeing me from roommates, and going into the summer before my junior year in college, I did a short stage at two-Michelin star restaurant, Lazy Bear, in San Francisco. The neat thing about Lazy Bear is that the restaurant actually started off as a pop-up restaurant and it is something they try to incorporate a lot into their food, ambiance, and philosophy. After the stage, I went to thinking about what I wanted to do for the rest of the summer. It didn't take too much time but I finally put things together and thought, "Shoot, I could run a pop-up restaurant out of my studio."

The rest of my summer was then spent carefully curating the experience I wanted guests to have at the pop-up. I tested dishes to put on the menu, went anywhere from thrift stores to three Michelin-starred restaurants to scavenge for plateware, glassware, silverware, and service pieces, sold my Boosted Board to buy kitchen equipment off Craigslist, figured out the layout and furniture to put in my studio that I had only seen pictures of, and spend hours sitting at my computer designing my menus and website. I had no idea how to do any of it, but I just learned as I went.

One of my proudest accomplishments was the carefully curated Spotify playlist for the restaurant that featured all my favorite classic 90's hip-hop and R&B with the likes of A Tribe Called Quest, Lauryn Hill, Wu-Tang Clan, Erykah Badu, and the Fugees. I wanted the experience at DENCH. to reflect who I was and the things that spoke to me most.

The pop-up was going to offer a multi-course tasting menu so that I could work on a lot of different dishes at once and allow for me to explore different techniques. I hoped the food would have integrity and represent who I was. Relying on my own cultural background and experiences, I tried combining the flavors that I grew up with and the techniques I learned working in restaurants to create unique and exciting dishes.

Once I had everything planned and mapped out, I packed my car and made my way back to school to get the whole thing started.

DENCH.

AFTER DOING A COUPLE TEST DINNERS, I announced the pop-up on my Instagram on September 17th, 2017 with this post: "POP-UP ALERT! I started a pop-up restaurant out of my studio in SLO! It's now open for reservations through 10/21. I serve a 5-7 course pre-fixe menu that showcases some of San Luis Obispo's finest seasonal and local produce. Trust me, bread and fish so good even Jesus would have eaten it before he could feed the 5,000. DENCH. is open Saturdays at 7pm and seats 4 people at a communal table. Grab three of your friends and make your reservation for undoubtedly one of the denchest meals of your life! Link to the restaurant reservation webpage in my bio! #dench".

Being real with you, I thought I was going to have to beg my friends to come eat at my place each week. You could then imagine my surprise, and excitement, to see that my first round of reservations booked out in just a couple of hours.

From the first reservation onwards, people seemed to be genuinely interested in what I was doing and the food I was serving. It was dope, I would know the person making the reservation but wouldn't know the people that they brought. Word then got out pretty quickly and soon an article about the pop-up appeared in the school paper. The headline read: "Aspiring chef opens high-class pop-up restaurant in apartment". It was pretty tight.

After the first quarter of doing the pop-up, I returned to my home in Cupertino where I did special pop-ups out of my parents' house serving an extended DENCH. tasting menu. That was the first time my parents were able to see me work in that kind of capacity and actually try my food. Now, I am pretty sure that my parents didn't understand my food at all, mostly because it wasn't stir-fried and served with rice, but I think they began to really see my passion for cooking and that it could actually take me somewhere. They accepted that I would be okay in life pursuing this passion even if I didn't end up as a lawyer or engineer.

The media flurry didn't really take off until I returned to school for the winter quarter of 2017. FoodBeast released an article about the pop-up and that's when DENCH. blew up. I'd wake up to a ton of emails of media requests from all different kinds of outlets. After doing interview after interview, I saw myself on places I never thought I'd see myself like NowThis, Insider, NextShark, international news outlets that I couldn't even read, and even on national TV when I got featured on ABC's *The Chew*. It was surreal to me how people from all over the world heard of my story and wanted to know more.

The last dinner I served was actually a pretty perfect way to end the school year. I had been contacted to host a pop-up for a party including the president of my university and his wife. I had always joked to my friends at the beginning of it all that I was going to one day serve President Armstrong at the pop-up and lo and behold, I found myself cooking dinner for him in my tiny studio apartment, Ice Cube blasting away in the background.

It was definitely tough trying to balance the pop-up, schoolwork, and a social life. Sometimes there wouldn't be a whole lot of separation between the three. I would spend lectures daydreaming about and doodling new dishes and make my friends hang out with me by asking them to taste test things I'd been working on. I'd spend the majority of each day thinking about ways to improve the pop-up.

There were a lot of times I thought to myself, "Man, working in an actual restaurant's going to be like this day in day out and the pop-up barely reaches the extent of the pressure I'd experience. Is this really what I want to do?" To be honest, it's still a question I ask myself often. It hurts sometimes to think about all of the sacrifices I see other chefs make in their personal lives in order to do what they love. Despite all this, there wasn't much else I'd rather be doing.

Before the school year wound down, I was given the opportunity to serve on the leadership team of my college fellowship, Asian American Christian Fellowship, for the next school year. Taking a larger role in the fellowship and serving on leadership had always been something on my heart going into Cal Poly from all of my experiences serving and doing ministry work in high school. What I saw in high school was how much my friends and the people around me in the Bay Area struggled with things like depression and self-worth. I would try to share God's love with people through a club I chartered—doing stuff like giving people bags of snacks, drinks, and encouraging notes during finals week or putting up banners around campus that read, "You are loved." This is something I saw Cal Poly could use too. I knew there was no way for me to do both the fellowship and pop-up at the same time and do them well so I had to decide between the two. I saw the merits to doing each of them, but thought back to the time I trusted God in my decision to stay at Cal Poly and what He was able to do through me and the pop-up because I stayed. I decided to once again put my faith in Him and turned down doing the pop-up in order to serve in my fellowship.

If you were one of the hundreds of people who kept asking me when I was going to open reservations or why I wasn't accepting reservations anymore this year…that's why.

My bad for swerving you guys. I'll cook for you at my future restaurant.

DENCH.

POP-UP RESTAURANT
September 9, 2017

croquette
serrano ham ~ cheese

milk bread
cultured butter

hamachi crudo
avocado ~ soy ~ nasturtium

lobster tail
pea ~ potato ~ lemon

intermezzo
citrus ~ honey

strawberry
basil ~ ivoire ~ chrysanthemum

mignardise
madeleine ~ bonbon ~ caramel
yunan pu-erh tea

DENCH

POP-UP RESTAURANT
September 9, 2017

croquette
serrano ham ~ cheese

milk bread
cultured butter

hamachi crudo
avocado ~ soy ~ nastu

lobster tail
pea ~ potato ~ le

interme
citrus ~ hor

straw
basil ~ ivo

mignardise
madeleine ~ bonbon ~ caramel
yunan pu-erh tea

THIS BOOK

THIS COOKBOOK was created as part of my senior project at Cal Poly. The entire time I spent documenting all of my recipes and techniques during the year of doing the pop-up, I knew I wanted to write a cookbook. I felt that a cookbook would be a cool way to share my experiences of doing DENCH. and get some sick pictures of the food too. I asked my friend Carly Lamera, a graphic communication major at Cal Poly, if she wanted to help me with the book. Luckily enough for me, she agreed and we spent our senior years in school photographing, writing, and designing this book.

All my menus had an illustration of a flower on it that either had to do with a garnish on a dish or the occasion of the night. The cover of the book is an illustration of all of the flowers that have appeared on my menus throughout the year.

The DENCH. cookbook features all of the different dishes I served during the course of the pop-up. Each of the recipes are also listed in the order that they made it onto the menu and are separated by the course in which they were served in. The recipes all start with a headnote explaining the background of the dish as well as sometimes lyrics from hip-hop songs I like. The pictures of all the dishes were also all shot on the same black table that guests ate at in my studio. All of the dishes are in some way an amalgamation of my experiences of eating and cooking ever since my childhood.

Many of the dishes in this book are going to be pretty hard to recreate in a home kitchen. The recipes in this book range pretty vastly in difficulty. They contain anywhere from one to nine different components that take multiple hours if not days of prep. All of the recipes are in metric which means that a scale is required. Many of the recipes also call for special ingredients and equipment. However, I do encourage you to try out and experiment with different aspects of dishes and explore new techniques!

That being said, happy cooking!

Or, you know, enjoy the pictures at least.

COURSE ONE

Canapé

CROQUETTE

My first job in a restaurant was bussing tables at a local Japanese restaurant. Without fail, the thing that they would always feed me for family meal was a Japanese potato croquette, known as a korokke, and rice. While I should have grown to hate these things, I honestly just couldn't get enough of these fried balls of potato. The croquettes I make are an homage to those frozen korokkes the restaurant used to feed my sixteen year-old self.

HAM & CHEESE CROQUETTE

200g cooked russet potato
20g heavy cream
3g thinly sliced scallions
white pepper
serrano ham
white cheddar
all-purpose flour
1 egg
panko bread crumbs
salt

Combine the potato, cream, and scallions together and mix until homogeneous. Season with salt and white pepper as desired. Using your hands, form the mixture into balls, stuffing them with small cubes of the white cheddar and slices of serrano ham. Once the balls have been formed, dredge the balls in flour, then egg, then panko bread crumbs. Fry the balls in neutral oil at 350°F until golden brown. Remove from the oil onto a wire rack and season with salt immediately.

LEMON AIOLI

1 egg
28g lemon juice
15g dijon mustard
224g canola oil
salt

Add everything together in an immersion blender cup and blend with a stick blender from bottom up slowly to emulsify all the ingredients together. Season as needed and reserve in a piping bag in the refrigerator.

PLATING

Pipe four, staggered dots of the aioli on the rectangular slate plate. Place the croquette balls on each of the dots. Pipe another dot of the aioli on top of the ball and top with microgreens. Serve immediately.

SHISHITO POPPER

I distinctly remember the smell of all the grilled shishito peppers wafting off people's plates at my favorite izakaya restaurant back home. I saw a bin full of these tasty Japanese peppers at the SLO farmers market one week and knew I had to have a dish with them on the menu. This is my take on a jalapeño popper: a tempura fried shishito pepper topped with whipped goat cheese on a bed of lime crema.

LIME CREMA

30g crème fraîche
5g lime juice
salt

Whisk together the crème fraîche and lime juice. Season to taste and reserve in the refrigerator.

WHIPPED BLACK TRUFFLE GOAT CHEESE

30g black truffle goat cheese
3g honey

Using a whisk, whip the goat cheese, slowly drizzling in the honey to taste, and continue to whip until light and fluffy.

TEMPURA BATTER

60g all-purpose flour
10g cornstarch
150g club soda

Whisk together dry ingredients before slowly whisking in the club soda until fully incorporated.

SHISHITO TEMPURA

4ea shishito pepper
tempura batter
1qt neutral oil
salt

Heat the oil to 350°F. Dry the shishito peppers and dip in the batter. Drain off any excess batter before dropping them into the oil. Fry until the batter becomes golden brown, about 3-4 minutes. Remove the peppers from the oil and allow to drain on kitchen paper. Salt the peppers.

PLATING

Place four spoonfuls of the crema on the slate. Pipe three dots of the goat cheese on top of the tempura. Sprinkle the togarashi and zest of a lemon on top of the tempura before placing them on the crema. Place wasabi microgreens on each goat cheese dot and serve.

STEAMED PACIFIC OYSTERS

Cantonese cuisine is mostly known for its clean flavors and dishes that highlight the pure essence of the protein or vegetable in the dish. Because Hong Kong is so close to the ocean, seafood is a huge mainstay in the cuisine. One of my favorite things to get at any Cantonese joint is steamed shellfish with soy, scallions, and cilantro. This dish is a local oyster steamed with xo sauce, another staple Cantonese condiment that consists of chili oil and dried seafood, topped with chives and the stems and leaves of cilantro.

STEAMED PACIFIC OYSTERS

4 pacific oysters
chives
xo sauce

Top the oysters with minced chives before steaming for 1 minute. Add a small dollop of xo sauce to the oyster before steaming for another 30 seconds.

PLATING

Top the oysters with lemon juice, cilantro leaves, and cilantro stems. Serve while oysters are still hot.

COURSE TWO

Bread

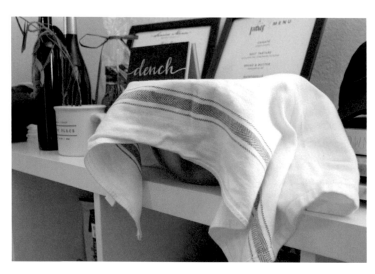

MILK BREAD

*"She finally played me, but yo I'd find another
'Cause I got the crazy game and yo,
I'm smooth like butter"*
Butter, A Tribe Called Quest

If I close my eyes and think about it, I can almost smell all the different breads on display in an Asian bakery. Whether it was scallions, char siu pork, hot dogs, custard, coconut, or taro, every item was encased in a sweet, Wonder Bread-like dough. The milk bread that I serve is reminiscent of the bread I grew up eating. Close to a parker house roll, this bread isn't super crusty or sour like traditional western bread, but damn, if it isn't soft, fluffy, and delicious. The bread is brushed with melted butter and topped with sea salt flakes and served with cultured butter.

MILK BREAD

Tangzhong:
92g milk
19g bread flour

Dough:
150g milk
25g sugar
7g active dry yeast
343g bread flour
10g salt
1 egg
15g butter

Heat the milk and sugar for the dough together to 110-115°F. Add yeast and let bloom for 10 minutes. In a pan, whisk together the 92g milk and 19g bread flour for the tangzhong in a pan on medium-low heat and continue whisking until mixture turns into a paste, then take it off heat. Bring all the ingredients for the bread dough together, including the tangzhong, minus the butter to the bowl of a stand mixer and knead for 6 minutes on a low speed in a stand mixer with the dough hook attachment. Add the butter and continue to knead for 7 min on a low speed. Grease a bowl and place dough inside, cover with a towel and proof for 1-1.5 hours. Divide into 6 rolls, 80g each. Flatten each roll with a rolling pin then roll the flattened dough into a pinwheel. Place the pinwheels into greased small loaf pans. Allow to proof for another 1-1.5 hours covered with a towel. Brush rolls with egg wash and bake at 350°F for 20 minutes. Remove the bread from the pan. Brush the tops with melted butter and sprinkle with maldon sea salt before serving.

PLATING

Serve the bread alongside a quenelle of cultured butter topped with maldon sea salt.

COURSE THREE

Pre-Entrée

KAMPACHI CRUDO

If ODB likes it raw, I guess I do too…fish that is. I remember when I was a kid my parents and friends would always bug out about eating raw fish but I could never get enough of it. Sashimi, poke, crudo…you name it, if it had raw fish in it, I was all over it. My crudo dish has slices of kampachi topped with shichimi togarashi, red onion, scallions, avocado purée, radish, and finished with a chilled citrus soy bonito broth.

AVOCADO PURÉE

1 small avocado
lemon juice
salt

Blend the flesh of the avocado together with just enough lemon juice to keep from oxidizing. Season with salt and reserve in a piping bag.

CITRUS SOY BONITO BROTH

235g water
8g bonito flakes
7g white soy sauce
10g lemon juice

Bring water and bonito flakes together in a pot and boil for 30 seconds. Strain the mixture into a container and cool. Once cool, add the lemon and soy.

PLATING

Arrange three slices of fish on the plate. Sprinkle shichimi togarashi over the fish. Pipe dots of the avocado purée around the fish. Place the radish slices, shaved red onion, julienned green onion, microgreens, and flower petals along the fish slices. Pour the citrus bonito broth over the fish in front of the guests and serve.

62°C TEA EGG

"How you like your eggs…"
Fried or Fertilized, Yung Humma
ft. Flynt Flossy

When coming up with my menus, I saw that chefs that I looked up to like David Chang or Alain Passard all had their own signature egg dishes so I figured I should probably have one too. I thought about the different egg dishes I've had growing up and the one that stuck out most to me was the Chinese tea egg. I remember my aunt dropping off pots of these ominous-looking brown eggs at my house and me excitedly coming home from school to devour them. Traditional Chinese tea eggs are hard boiled eggs that have been steeped in a soy and tea marinade. The eggs are steeped for an extended period of time so that the egg can take on the color of the marinade as the flavor of it permeates through to the core of the egg. Not a fan of the hard, chalky yolk of the traditional tea egg, I looked to do a dish around a runny yolked tea egg. What I settled on was a technique developed by Modernist Cuisine and involved an egg that is cooked in three different stages. My egg dish became an iconic one and features a 62°C egg steeped in lapsang souchong, a smoked black tea, and served with Chinese red vinegar, scallions, oyster mushrooms, and a stick of toasted brioche.

62°C TEA EGG

For 6 eggs

Boil the eggs for 4 minutes 20 seconds then immediately shock in an ice bath for 15 minutes. Put eggs into a sous vide bath at 62°C for 30 min before shocking in an ice bath again for 15 minutes. Crack egg shells with the back of a spoon to create a spiderweb pattern. Leave the eggs in the soak for at least 12 hours in the refrigerator. Peel the eggs, submerging them in a bowl of water, before placing in a plastic heat proof bag. When ready to serve, bring the eggs back up to temperature in a sous vide bath at 62°C for 25 minutes.

TEA EGG SOAK

600g water
35g dark soy sauce
35g light soy sauce
2 star anise pods
65g rock sugar
12g lapsang souchong

Bring ingredients together in large pot and bring to a boil and reduce to about 400g of liquid. Strain into a container and cool.

PLATING

Place a bundle of julienned scallions into the corner of the bowl. Next to the scallions, place the egg, pointed side facing the front of the bowl. Shingle the sautéed trumpet mushroom slices under the scallions. Using a paring knife, cut into the egg and allow for the yolk to run. Drizzle the red vinegar behind the egg as well as into the pool of yolk. Top the egg with the brioche baton and serve.

THE TEMPERATURE PROGRESSION OF THE 62° TEA EGG

INTRODUCTION

In addition to this cookbook, part of my senior project at Cal Poly was also to conduct some food science testing on my tea egg dish. Under the instruction of Dr. Samir Amin, I ended up doing tracking the progression of the egg yolk's temperature throughout the entire cook process of the dish. This spread is loosely designed to mimic what my experiment would look like in an actual scientific journal.

MATERIALS & METHOD

The temperature profile of the egg was taken by first vacuum sealing the grade AA, large-sized eggs in separate bags. The top of the eggshells were then punctured through the bag with a small needle where a thermocouple inserted through some sous vide tape before it was placed through the hole in the eggshell. The tape was then secured to the outside of the bag to hold the thermocouple in place in the egg yolk. The thermocouples were programmed to take a reading of the internal temperature of the egg every ten seconds. The eggs were then cooked according to the directions of the dish: first boiled for four minutes twenty seconds, then shocked in an ice bath for twenty minutes, then cooked in an immersion circulator at 62°C for thirty minutes, then shocked in an ice bath until the internal temperature of the egg reached 4°C, the same temperature as a household refrigerator, then finally put back into the immersion circulator for twenty-five minutes.

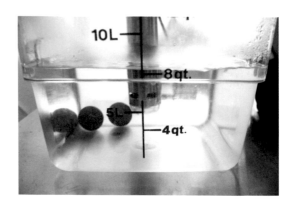

TEMPERATURE PROGRESSION OF 62° TEA EGG

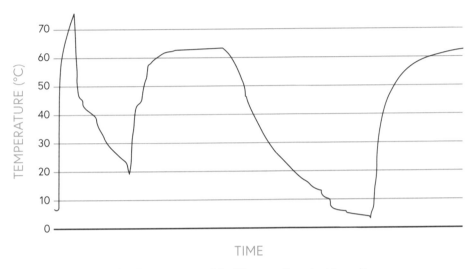

Fig. 1 Heating and cooling progression of the 62° tea egg throughout its cooking process

RESULTS & DISCUSSION

Another part of my senior project was to write a literature review compiling a few different source materials, research articles, and journals on the topic of eggs, egg proteins, and sous vide cooking. I won't bore you with the whole lit review but through all my research and reading, it is important to point out that the two main variables in cooking shell-on eggs, especially sous vide, is time and temperature. Both of these variables play a role in the final texture of the egg. For example, an egg that is cooked at the same temperature, even if the water isn't boiling, let's say for example 60°C, the texture of the egg will be noticeably different when pulled at forty-five minutes compared to an hour and a half, or even six hours. At forty-five minutes, both the egg white and yolk are incredibly runny whereas a six hour egg has a much less loose white with an almost solid yolk. This is much different than most things that are cooked sous vide. A medium-rare steak, at 54°C, would retain it's doneness in an immersion circulator for up to four hours without diminishing in quality. So when restaurants call their eggs a 62°C or 63°C or 64°C egg, there isn't quite a standard for that. Since the eggs can vary so much texturally due to the time of cooking, even if they are at the same temperature, it would be rather irresponsible to declare what exactly a 62°C or 63°C or 64°C egg is.

The temperature progression the eggs in my dish go through during the cook process is shown through Figure 1, where it's shown in a scatter plot chart. In the initial stage of boiling, the internal temperature of the egg goes from around 6°C to all the way up to 75°C briefly until the eggs hit the first ice bath. In the first bath, the eggs are cooled to around 20°C before they are dropped into the 62°C sous vide bath. The eggs hit 62°C in approximately fifteen minutes where it stays constant at that temperature for another fifteen minutes. The eggs are then shocked in an ice bath until it reaches 4°C, the same temperature of a refrigerator to emulate the process of marinating the eggs in the tea/soy marinade the fridge. Then after the eggs are placed in the final sous vide bath, it takes about twenty minutes for the egg to come back to 62°C where it stays at that temperature for another five minutes until the egg is served.

The graph isn't the smoothest due to the thermocouples being slightly moved at times due to the boiling water or water bath. However, the graph does give a pretty good glimpse into what it's like to be an egg for my dish. The boiling stage proved to give the egg its most rapid heating experience while the immersion bath cooks gave the eggs more of an expected gentle heating where it tapered off when the egg reached the same temperature as the water bath.

CONCLUSION

The temperature journey the egg takes to becoming my tea egg is pretty exciting. Also, since there isn't really such a thing as a 62°C egg, I guess I should figure out a new name for the dish.

COURSE FOUR

Main Course

LOBSTER TAIL

"Feed you lobster 'cause I'm a true mobster"
I Need You Tonight, Junior M.A.F.I.A.

My mom thinks lobster is only delicious when first fried, then stir fried with ginger and scallions. I think otherwise. There are few things more compatible than lobster and butter. This dish is made up of a butter poached lobster tail, pea purée, potato purée, and some prosciutto curls.

LOBSTER TAILS

4 lobster tails
butter
tarragon
chives
lemon

Bring a pot of water to a full boil. Insert 2 skewers between the top of the shell and the meat in the lobster tails. Boil the lobster tails for 1 minute before shocking in an ice bath. Crack and peel the shell, leaving the meat fully intact. Bag the lobster meat with butter and sprigs of tarragon. Cook in a water bath at 54°C for 30 minutes. Remove the tails from the bag and top with minced chives and lemon zest.

PEA PURÉE

200g frozen peas
butter
salt

Thaw the frozen peas by submerging them in water. Blend the peas together with a small amount of water to get them flowing. Once puréed, strain the purée into a pot. Heat the purée in the pot before seasoning with salt and finishing with butter.

POTATO PURÉE

400g potato
200g butter
111g milk, whole
4g salt

Heat a sous vide bath to 90°C. Peel and small dice the potatoes. Bag the potatoes together with the butter, milk, and salt. Cook in water bath for 60 minutes or until tender. Pass all ingredients through a tammis and emulsify together. Adjust for seasoning.

PLATING

Place the lobster tail onto the plate. Next to the lobster tail, place alternating spoonfuls of the pea and potato purées. Arrange pea shoots and rolls of prosciutto onto the purées and serve.

FIVE SPICE DUCK BREAST

I'll go ahead and say it: Cantonese barbecue is the unequivocal king of all international barbecue styles. Both my parents grew up in Hong Kong where Cantonese barbecue hawker stalls filled the busy streets. I remember every single special occasion in the family would result in styrofoam boxes of crispy roast pork, sweet barbecued pork char siu, soy sauce chicken, and my favorite roast duck finding its way onto the dining room table. This dish is a nod to all those roast ducks I devoured as a kid: a five-spiced duck breast topped with a scallion salad and served alongside a seasonal plum sauce.

DUCK BREAST

4 duck breasts
salt
five spice
white pepper

The night before cooking, rub the duck breasts with the salt, five spice, and white pepper and allow to sit uncovered in the refrigerator overnight. Bag the breasts and cook in an immersion bath at 54°C for 45 minutes. Remove from the bath and dry each breast before searing using your preferred method.

PLUM SAUCE

350g plums
15g light soy sauce
5g mirin
5g rice wine vinegar
70g red onion
1g red chili flake
15g ginger
10g garlic
15g sugar
1g citric acid

Bring all ingredients together in a small saucepan. Cook the ingredients on medium-high down to a jammy consistency, about 5-10 minutes. Then immersion blend together the sauce directly in the saucepan to combine. Sieve the mixture and cool. Reserve in the refrigerator.

SCALLION SALAD

scallions
sesame oil
gochugaru
roasted white sesame seeds

Julienne the greens of the scallions and shock in an ice bath until curled. Dry the scallions before tossing to coat with sesame oil. Season with the gochugaru and sesame seeds and reserve.

PLATING

Slice the duck breast. Place the breast onto the plate before piping dots of the plum sauce next to the duck. Dust five spice over and off to the side of the breast. Top the breast with a bundle of the scallion salad. Add pieces of fresh pluots onto the plum sauce dots and serve.

BEEF RIBEYE

"I like beef and broccoli, motherf-----."
Beef and Broccoli, Immortal Technique

This is my play on the classic Chinese American takeout item: beef and broccoli. Slices of beef ribeye served with a creamy broccoli purée, sautéed broccolini, oyster sauce gastrique, and pickled red onion petals.

BEEF RIBEYE

beef ribeye
salt
butter

Vacuum pack the ribeye steak and cook in an immersion circulator set at 54°C for 45 minutes. Remove from the bath and pat completely dry. Season each side liberally with salt before searing using your desired method. Finish the steak by basting it with butter.

BROCCOLI PURÉE

500g broccoli
100g water
90g butter
5g salt
white pepper

Steam all the ingredients together in pot until the broccoli is tender. Emulsify together with a stick blender. Add additional butter as needed. When completely emulsified, season the purée as needed with additional salt and white pepper.

OYSTER SAUCE GASTRIQUE

32g oyster sauce
12g soy sauce
5g rice wine vinegar
6g sugar
cornstarch

Combine the oyster sauce, soy sauce, rice wine vinegar, and sugar together in pot and heat to boil. Make a slurry with cornstarch and water. Slowly whisk in the slurry into the sauce and thicken to the desired consistency.

PICKLED PEARL ONION PETALS

100g water
100g white wine vinegar
20g sugar
5g salt
1g black peppercorns
pearl red onion

Whisk all the ingredients minus the pearl onions together until dissolved. Pour the brine over separated quartered pearl red onion petals and let sit for at least 90 minutes. Reserve the petals in brine until needed.

PLATING

Place two slices of the ribeye in the center of the plate, slightly staggered. Spoon a circle of the oyster sauce gastrique next to the steak at the top of the plate. Using a spoon, place two dollops of the broccoli purée on each side of the steak. Place the sautéed broccolini alongside the steak, on top of the purée. Top the steak slices with the pickled pearl red onion petals and micro-greens and serve.

PORK TENDERLOIN

People normally freak out whenever they see that their pork has even a touch pink on it but the honest best way to enjoy pork is mid rare. I thought this dish of a pork tenderloin, crispy prosciutto, prosciutto curls, hoisin sauce, and baby bok choy would be pretty tasty. Turns out I was pretty bang on.

BOK CHOY

baby bok choy
mushroom stock
salt

Wash and dry the baby bok choy before cutting in half lengthwise. Season the bok choy before lightly searing the flat side of the vegetable. Add the mushroom stock and let braise until tender.

CRISPY PROSCIUTTO SHARDS

prosciutto

Cut the prosciutto into same-sized, but irregular shaped pieces. Place the prosciutto between two pieces of kitchen paper and microwave for ~20 seconds. Remove and allow to air dry. The prosciutto should turn opaque and crispy.

PORK TENDERLOIN

pork tenderloin
garlic
thyme
salt
white pepper

Vacuum pack the pork tenderloin with garlic cloves and thyme. Cook in an immersion circulator set at 54°C for 1 hour. Remove the tenderloin from the bag and pat dry. Season with salt and white pepper before searing on all sides using your desired method.

ROASTED ONION

white pearl onions
butter
salt

Peel and cut the top and bottom off the onions. Melt butter in an oven-safe pan over medium heat and add onions. Coat onions with butter and season with salt. Place the pan in a 325°F oven for 30 minutes, flipping the onions every 5 minutes.

PLATING

Place the bok choy half in the center of the plate. Arrange two slices of the pork tenderloin alongside the bok choy. Pipe dots of hoisin sauce next to the tenderloin slices. Add the roasted onion before placing the prosciutto curls on either side of the bok choy. Add the crispy prosciutto along the bok choy then finish with microgreens.

COURSE FIVE

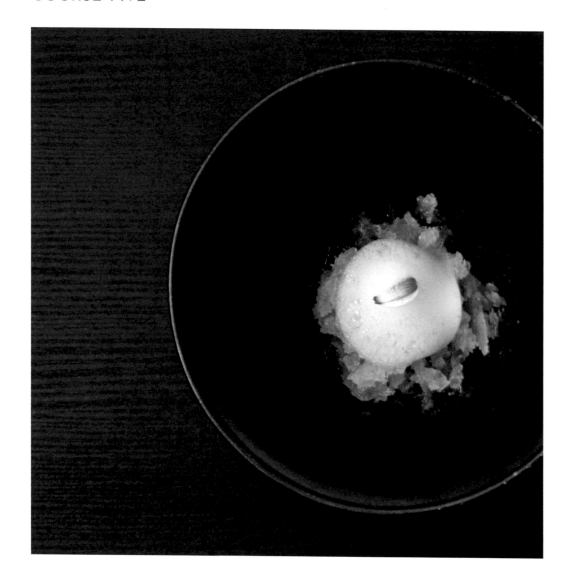

Intermezzo

INTERMEZZO

This intermezzo is served after the savory courses are finished to cleanse the palate before the dessert courses. The base of the course is the granita that would change according to the seasonal fruit available—which is why you see three different intermezzos in the pictures. Fall - pomegranate, winter - pomelo, spring - strawberry. The intermezzo features an icy fruit granita topped with a chewy honey tapioca and finished with a light, airy lemon foam.

FOAM

75g fruit juice
50g simple syrup
125g water
2g soy lecithin

Combine ingredients together and blend with an immersion blender until foam forms and stabilizes.

GRANITA

400g water
125g sugar
1.25g gold leaf gelatin
250g fruit juice

Heat half the water and all of the sugar to simmer in a saucepan. Bloom the gelatin in cold water before adding to the water and sugar and dissolving. Add the rest of the water and juice and pour into a freezer-safe container. Freeze until solid then scrape the surface with a fork to create the granita. Reserve in the freezer.

HONEY TAPIOCA

30g tapioca
100g simple syrup
4g honey

Cover the tapioca in water in a saucepan and bring to a boil. Immediately pour the tapioca through a sieve and rinse under cold water. Place tapioca back in the saucepan and cover with water again and boil for 8-10 minutes or until translucent and al dente. Again, pour the tapioca through a sieve and rinse under cold water. Drain the water from the tapioca. Add the honey to the simple syrup and heat gently until the honey has dissolved. Add the tapioca to the honey/simple syrup and reserve in the refrigerator.

SIMPLE SYRUP

200g water
200g sugar

Add the sugar and water together in a saucepan and mix until combined. Bring the mixture to a boil for 5 seconds before pouring into a container and allowing to cool.

PLATING

Place a large spoonful of the granita on the bottom of the bowl. Then top with the tapioca along with some of the liquid the tapioca was in. Top with a spoonful of the foam and then finally the edible flower petal. Serve.

COURSE SIX

Dessert

BASIL PANNA COTTA

The basil panna cotta was the first dessert I put on the menu. To be honest, the only reason it was the first was because my first diners had all sorts of dietary restrictions that didn't let me use all my favorite summer fruits. Basil is especially fragrant in the summertime and I had always thought using basil for sweet applications was super interesting. This basil panna cotta is topped with a whipped white chocolate ganache, fresh strawberry, macerated strawberry, chrysanthemum gelée, and basil meringue.

BASIL MERINGUE

See pg 93.

BASIL POWDER

See pg 92.

BASIL PANNA COTTA

680g cream
75g sugar
3ea gelatin sheets (gold)
2 bunch basil

Bloom gelatin in cold water. Bring the cream, sugar, basil together in a saucepan and bring to a boil. Turn off the heat before covering saucepan and letting steep for 5 minutes. Immersion blend all ingredients together then pass through a sieve. Add in the bloomed gelatin and stir to dissolve. Cast into bowls and let set overnight in fridge.

CHRYSANTHEMUM GELÉE

120g water
12g sugar
1.2g agar
1g chrysanthemum tea

Bring the water and tea to a boil. Remove from heat and cover. Let steep for 15 minutes. Sieve the tea to another saucepan and shear in the agar mixed with the sugar. Bring to a boil for at least 15 seconds then cast into a container. Allow to cool and fully set.

MACERATED STRAWBERRY

See pg 92.

WHIPPED IVOIRE GANACHE

65g 35% white chocolate
35g cream

Heat the cream in a small saucepan to a bare simmer. Pour the cream over the chocolate and emulsify together. Pour into a container and allow to cool and crystallize. When needed, whip the ganache until fluffy and reserve in a piping bag with a ruffle piping tip.

PLATING

Off to one side of the panna cotta, pipe a ribbon of the ivoire ganache. On the other side of the panna cotta, dust some basil powder. On the ganache, place pieces of fresh strawberry, broken up pieces of the chrysanthemum gelée, and spoonfuls of the macerated strawberry. Top the ganache with two pieces of the basil meringue. Finish garnishing with micro basil leaves and serve.

PEACH MOUSSE

I would like to think that Snoop and I share the same appreciation for stone fruit season. With the abundance of peaches, nectarines, and plums that flood the San Luis Obispo farmers markets during the summer and early fall, I knew I wanted to create a dish around one of my favorite fruits. This was my take on peaches and cream and was one of the first desserts I put out in the pop-up.

PEACH MOUSSE

275g cream
145g peach juice
5g lemon juice
40g sugar

Whip the cream in a stand mixer until soft peaks form, then shear in sugar and beat until stiff peaks. Fold in the juices into the whipped cream until homogeneous. Spread flat onto a acetate-lined sheet pan then freeze. Once frozen, cut out circles of the mousse using a circle cutter and transfer to the final plate. Allow to thaw in the refrigerator until needed.

VANILLA CRÈME CHANTILLY

150g heavy cream
20g sugar
½ vanilla pod

Combine heavy cream with the seeds from half a vanilla pod and beat until soft peaks before shearing in sugar and beating until stiff peaks have formed. Place the crème chantilly into a container and reserve in the fridge.

MERINGUE TUBES

See pg 93.

SORBET SYRUP

See pg 92.

PEACH SORBET

490g yellow peach juice
10g lemon juice
200g sorbet syrup

Blend all ingredients together with an immersion blender until homogeneous and allow to chill overnight. Spin in an ice cream machine according to manufacturer's instructions.

PEACH FLUID GEL

100g peach juice
5g lemon juice
10g simple syrup
ultra-tex 3 modified tapioca starch

Mix juices and simple syrup together in a container. Add the modified tapioca starch, a spoonful at a time, and blend with an immersion blender until a pipeable consistency is reached.

ALMOND TUILE

90g sugar
60g egg white
2g vanilla extract
1g salt
23g all-purpose flour
30g melted unsalted butter
sliced almonds

Whisk together the sugar, egg white, and vanilla. Add the flour and salt and mix well. Then add the melted butter and mix until combined. Drop spoonfuls of the tuile batter onto a silicone baking mat and spread thin using the back of the spoon. Sprinkle the sliced almonds over the flattened batter discs. Bake at 400°F for 8 minutes or until golden brown. Once out of the oven, punch out circles of the tuile using a circle cutter. Allow to cool and harden before storing in an airtight container with silica desiccant packets.

PLATING

Place half a spoonful of crushed meringue in between the three mounds of mousse. Spoon a quenelle of the crème chantilly and peach sorbet on top of the crushed meringue. Pipe dots of the peach gel around the mousse before laying the slices of the compressed peaches. Dust peach powder on each of the mousse mounds. Then lay the meringue tubes and almond tuiles along the sides of the mousse, sorbet, and crème chantilly.

JASMINE POACHED PEAR

I have this distinct memory of my mom making me this sweet soup of Asian pear and ginger for dessert in the fall. But after I called her asking for the recipe, she informed me that she had never made anything like that for me before. I honestly don't know where I have this memory from. Regardless, I made a dessert from it adding some additional fall flavors with cinnamon and playing around with multiple temperatures. The dessert is a jasmine poached pear, in a ginger pear consommé, with a cinnamon tuile, and ginger ice cream.

JASMINE POACHED PEAR

2 bosc pears
705g strongly brewed jasmine tea
75g sugar
small 1 inch piece of ginger

Add the ginger, tea, and sugar into pot and bring to boil. Reduce the heat to medium and simmer for 5 minutes. Peel, core, and cut pears in half and place in a single layer face down into the liquid. Add a cartouche over the top of the pears. Simmer gently for 15-20 minutes or until the pears are tender, make sure to occasionally spoon the hot liquid over pears. Reserve the pears in the liquid to cool. Gently reheat the pears in the liquid when needed.

PEAR CONSOMMÉ

343g pear juice
15g ginger juice
6g simple syrup

Combine the liquids together and store in refrigerator.

CINNAMON TUILE

28g butter
25g light b. sugar
30g corn syrup
16g all-purpose flour
0.65g cinnamon
salt

Melt butter, brown sugar, corn syrup together in pot. Stir the dry ingredients into the melted mixture and whisk together until no lumps remain. Spread thin on silpat and bake at 375°F for 8 minutes. Allow to cool completely before breaking off into shards. Store in an airtight container with silica desiccant packets.

GINGER ICE CREAM

71g ginger
476g cream
240g milk, whole
100g sugar
6 yolks
salt

Peel and slice the ginger very thinly. Cover the ginger strands with water in a saucepan and boil for 1 min. Drain the ginger before adding to the cream/milk, half of the sugar, and salt. Bring to a bare simmer. Turn off the heat and cover and let infuse for 30-45 min. In a separate bowl, whisk yolks with other half of the sugar. Bring the cream mixture back up to a bare simmer. Temper 1.5 cups of the mixture into the yolks, ½ cup at a time. Pour tempered mixture back into saucepan and heat for 1-2 min longer or until the mixture coats the back of a spoon. Strain into a container and chill base overnight before spinning in an ice cream machine.

PLATING

Pour in the consommé into the base of the bowl. Place the warm poached pear in the center of the bowl. Top the pear with the cinnamon tuile. Add diced Asian pear to the center of the tuile. Add a quenelle of the ice cream on top of the diced pear. Finish with flower petals and serve.

THAI BASIL ICE CREAM

I suppose I didn't realize it until now, but this dish was heavily influenced by Massimo Bottura's *Oops! I Dropped the Lemon Tart* dessert at Osteria Francescana in Modena, Italy. I wanted to create an ice cream dessert that had tuiles surrounding it, sort of like a gift that the guest had to open to find the contents of. The dish was created in the winter time where the citrus season was booming in SLO and meyer lemons were aplenty. I'd always loved the flavors of citrus, basil, and coconut together, so to create a dish like this was a ton of fun. The dish features a meyer lemon curd, meyer lemon gel, toasted coconut chips, thai basil ice cream, coconut powder, meyer lemon zest, all surrounded by some tuiles. Side note: this is my favorite dish that I ever put out on the menu.

THAI BASIL ICE CREAM

476g cream
180g milk, 2%
100g sugar
20 torn thai basil leaves
5 egg yolks, large
salt, to taste

Add the cream, milk, salt, and 50g of sugar into a saucepan and heat over medium-high heat. When mixture begins to simmer gently, add the basil and stir. When the mixture begins to simmer again, remove the saucepan from the heat and cover. Let the mixture steep for about 20 minutes or until it is fragrant and sweet. Whisk the yolks and remaining sugar together in a heatproof bowl. Uncover the saucepan containing the infused cream and heat on medium until mixture reaches a bare simmer. Temper 1 cup of the mixture into the yolks in the heatproof bowl, ½ cup at a time. Pour tempered mixture back into saucepan and heat for 1-2 min longer. Strain the ice cream base into a container and chill base overnight before spinning using your desired method.

COCONUT POWDER

See pg 92.

LEMON GEL

75g lemon juice
50g simple syrup
125g water
ultra-tex 3 modified tapioca starch

Mix all the liquids together in a container. Add the modified tapioca starch, a spoonful at a time, and blend with an immersion blender until a pipeable consistency is reached.

SABLE TUILE

120g unsalted butter
120g sugar
120g egg white
5g vanilla
1g salt
120g all-purpose flour

Cream the butter and sugar together in a stand mixer. Add the egg whites, one at a time, while the mixer is on a low speed and allow to emulsify completely before adding the next white. Add vanilla and mix. Fold in the flour and salt. Spread the batter thin on silpat and bake at 400°F for 10 minutes or until light brown. Allow the tuile to cool before breaking into shards. Store in an airtight container along with silica desiccant packets.

MEYER LEMON CURD

75g meyer lemon juice
5g lemon zest
100g unsalted butter
88g sugar
4 egg yolks
2.5g citric acid
0.5g salt

Place all the ingredients into a bag and cook in an immersion circulator at 75°C for 1 hour. Pour the contents of the bag into a blender and blend together until emulsified, 30–60 seconds. Allow to cool and reserve in the refrigerator.

PLATING

Pipe the lemon curd into the middle of the plate. Around the curd, pipe three dots of the lemon gel around the curd. Top the curd with toasted coconut. Add a scoop of the thai basil ice cream on top of the toasted coconut. Encase the ice cream with three sablé tuile shards, placed between the lemon gel dots. Place a micro basil leaf on each of the lemon gel dots. Top the dessert with coconut powder and meyer lemon zest and serve.

GRAND MARNIER SOUFFLÉ

One of the first tasks given to me at when I arrived at The Plumed Horse was buttering and sugaring ramekins for soufflés. I remember meticulously using a pastry brush to spread a perfect, even layer of butter all along the walls and bottom of the ramekin before filling them with sugar and rotating to coat. Soufflés are one of the most classic French desserts and found its way onto my menu for a special Valentine's pop-up dinner.

GRAND MARNIER CRÈME ANGLAISE

1 egg yolk
120g cream
33g sugar
8g grand marnier
3g vanilla paste
3g orange zest

Whisk the ingredients minus the orange zest together in a small saucepan. Heat on medium, constantly stirring, until thickened enough to coat the back of a spatula. Remove from heat and stir in the orange zest before allowing to cool completely. Cover the surface of the crème anglaise with cling film and reserve in the refrigerator.

GRAND MARNIER SOUFFLÉ

Four 5oz Soufflés:
48g butter + more for ramekins
48g all-purpose flour
114g milk, whole
4 yolks
3g orange zest
2g vanilla extract
30g grand marnier
4 egg whites
100g sugar + more for ramekins

Brush the insides of four, 5 oz ramekins and coat with sugar. In a pan, heat the flour and butter to make a roux before adding in the milk and whisking to combine. Allow to thicken slightly over the heat. Cook the mixture until it lifts away from the pan. Move the mixture to a mixing bowl. Add the egg yolks, zest, vanilla and grand marnier to the bowl and mix together until homogeneous. In a separate bowl, whisk the egg whites with sugar to soft peaks. Fold the egg whites into the egg yolk mixture. Using a piping bag, fill the ramekins with the soufflé batter and level off using an offset spatula. Using your thumb, scrape alongside the edge of the ramekin to create an indentation and clean off the edges. Bake the soufflés on a tray at 400°F for 14 minutes.

PLATING

Place the soufflé on a doily-lined plate. At the table, create a hole in the center of the soufflé using a spoon and pour the chilled crème anglaise into the opening. Pause to enjoy the beautiful sight before enjoying.

RAEKWON'S ICE CREAM

"French-vanilla, butter-pecan,
chocolate-deluxe
Even caramel sundaes is gettin' touched
And scooped in my ice cream truck,
Wu tears it up"
Ice Cream, Raekwon

Raekwon's *Ice Cream* off of his debut album, *Only Built 4 Cuban Linx*, is one of my favorite songs of all time. Raekwon's da Chef…I'm kind of, sort of a chef…It was basically a match made in heaven. I'd always wanted to do a dessert around the flavors mentioned in the hook of the song. What I ended up with is a quenelle of chocolate deluxe ice cream next to a chocolate crémeux, cocoa dusted meringue, butter pecan croquants, and topped with a French vanilla crème chantilly and cherry powder.

CHOCOLATE DELUXE ICE CREAM

5 yolks
150g sugar
21g high quality cocoa
227g milk, 2%
397g cream
salt

Whisk together yolks and half of the sugar in a bowl and set aside. Add cocoa powder to a saucepan and whisk in the milk, little at a time, until a paste forms. Whisk in the rest of the milk, rest of the sugar, cream, and a pinch of salt. Bring the cocoa powder, cream, and milk mixture up to bare simmer. Temper 1.5 cups of the cream/milk into egg yolks, ½ cup at a time. Pour mixture back into saucepan and heat for 1-2 min longer or until the mixture coats the back of a spoon. Strain into container and chill overnight before spinning in an ice cream machine.

VANILLA CRÈME CHANTILLY

150g heavy cream
20g sugar
5g vanilla paste

Combine heavy cream with vanilla paste in a bowl and whisk until aerated before shearing in sugar and beating until the whipped cream is just under the soft peak stage. Use immediately.

COCOA DUSTED MERINGUE

See pg 93.

BUTTER PECAN CROQUANT

50g glucose syrup
50g sugar
125g water
pecans
butter powder

Heat the sugar and water until dissolved. Add glucose syrup and cook until mixture reaches 145°C. Pour mixture onto silpat and allow to harden. Once hard, break into small pieces and blitz in a spice grinder until a fine powder forms. Dust the powder in an even layer onto a silpat and top with crushed pecans. Bake at 350°F for 8 minutes. Once out of the oven, dust with butter powder while the warm and wait until cool to remove the croquant. Break croquants into shards and store in an airtight container with a silica desiccant packet.

GUANAJA CRÉMEUX

50g cream
50g milk, whole
1 yolk
10g sugar
48g 70% dark chocolate

Whisk together the yolk and sugar in a bowl. In a saucepan, heat the cream and milk to a boil. Temper the cream and milk mixture into the yolk and sugar mixture. Bring back the tempered mixture to the saucepan and heat to 86°C. Melt the chocolate in double boiler. Cool the crème anglaise to 50°C. Add the anglaise into the melted chocolate and emulsify together. Strain into a container and cool until set.

PLATING

Place a spoonful of crushed meringue into the center of the bowl. Place a quenelle of the chocolate ice cream on top of the crushed meringue. On one side of the ice cream, pipe dots of the crémeux, alternating with the cocoa dusted meringue kisses. Place a croquant in each of the crémeux dots. Top the ice cream with the soft whipped crème chantilly off to the other side of the ice cream. Dust with freeze-dried cherry powder and serve.

GUANAJA GANACHE

First popularized by Alinea, a wildly-famous Chicago restaurant known for their avant-garde cooking techniques, I always thought flexi ganache was the coolest thing ever. The chocolate components on this dish were to complement and highlight the different textures and preparations of the strawberries. This dish was created right when strawberry season was hitting its stride in San Luis Obispo where we are the home of the only strawberry-focused research center in the country. The dish is a piece of Guanaja flexi ganache topped with a Guanaja crémeux, fresh strawberries, freeze dried strawberries, macerated strawberries, strawberry meringue, crunchy chocolate pearls, and jasmine gelée.

GUANAJA FLEXI GANACHE

65g 70% chocolate, melted
180g cream
23g invert sugar
13g glucose
1g salt
0.4g agar
1.5g gelatin

Combine the cream, invert sugar, glucose, salt, and agar in pot and bring to boil for 1 minute. Add bloomed gelatin to the cream mixture and dissolve. Pour the hot cream mixture onto chocolate and let sit for 1 minute. Emulsify together with a heatproof spatula. Pour the ganache into an acetate-lined 8"x10" pan. Let the ganache cool for at least 2 hours then refrigerate until fully set. Cut ganache into the desired shape.

MACERATED STRAWBERRY

See pg 92.

GUANAJA CRÉMEUX

50g cream
50g milk, whole
1 yolk
10g sugar
48g 70% dark chocolate

Whisk together the yolk and sugar in a bowl. In a saucepan, heat the cream and milk to a boil. Temper the cream and milk mixture into the yolk and sugar mixture. Bring back the tempered mixture to the saucepan and heat to 86°C. Melt the chocolate in double boiler. Cool the crème anglaise to 50°C. Add the anglaise into the melted chocolate and emulsify together. Strain into a container and cool until set.

JASMINE GELÉE

120g water
12g sugar
1.2g agar
1g jasmine tea leaves

Bring the water and tea to a boil. Remove from heat and cover. Let steep for 15 minutes. Sieve the tea to another saucepan and shear in the agar mixed with the sugar. Bring to a boil for at least 15 seconds then cast into a container. Allow to cool and fully set.

STRAWBERRY MERINGUE

See pg 93.

PLATING

Place the flexi ganache onto the plate. Pipe 5 alternating dots of the crémeux on the ganache. Place slices of the fresh strawberries between each crémeux dot. Add pieces of the freeze dried strawberry and macerated strawberry onto the ganache. Break up pieces of the jasmine gelée and place on the ganache. Top with crunchy chocolate pearls and pieces of the strawberry meringue. To finish, add the flower petals and serve.

WATERMELON CONSOMMÉ

This was the dessert I served to the president of my university, his wife, the CEO, and VP of the largest beer distributors in the Central Coast. Flavorwise, this is probably the most "out there" dessert I've served. Summer was just beginning and I wanted to capture the smells and tastes I remember from my summers as a kid. This dessert is a watermelon sorbet in a watermelon cucumber consommé with mint olive oil topped with an olive oil powder, bee pollen, and mint.

WATERMELON CUCUMBER CONSOMMÉ

400g watermelon juice
25g cucumber juice
35g simple syrup
spearmint leaves

Combine juices and syrup together. Tear spearmint leaves and let infuse in the juices in the fridge at least overnight.

COMPRESSED WATERMELON

watermelon
sherry vinegar

Cut ¼ inch slices of watermelon and place them in a vacuum seal bag. Add a drizzle of the sherry vinegar to the bag and vacuum seal in a chamber vacuum sealer. The watermelon should be a deep red and nearly translucent.

WATERMELON SORBET

500g watermelon juice
200g sorbet syrup

Mix the watermelon juice and sorbet syrup together and let chill overnight in the refrigerator. Spin in an ice cream machine according to the manufacturer's instructions. Transfer the sorbet to a container and allow to harden in the freezer.

SORBET SYRUP

See pg 92.

OLIVE OIL POWDER

See pg 92.

WATERMELON MINT ESPUMA

250g watermelon juice
25g simple syrup
6 large torn spearmint leaves
6.2g 170 bloom gelatin

Combine the juice and simple syrup with the spearmint leaves and let infuse for at least 4 hours. Strain the mixture and transfer 69g of juice to small saucepan and let the gelatin bloom in the juice. Once bloomed, heat the juice on low heat until the gelatin is completely dissolved. Add the rest of strained juice to saucepan and chill over ice until cold and viscous. Add the mixture to a whipping siphon and charge 3 times with nitrous oxide. Store the siphon in the refrigerator until needed.

MINT INFUSED OLIVE OIL

65g extra virgin olive oil
3g torn mint leaves

Combine the oil and mint in a small saucepan and heat over low heat for 10 minutes. Take off the heat and allow to sit together overnight before straining.

PLATING

Pour the consommé into a chilled bowl. Place a square of compressed watermelon into the center of the bowl. Top the watermelon slice with a scoop of watermelon sorbet. Top the sorbet with the olive oil powder. Garnish with mint, bee pollen, and flower petals. Drizzle the mint infused olive oil into the consommé and serve.

MINI BAKED ALASKA

People love free stuff. People especially love free stuff on their birthday. This was my free stuff on people's birthdays. The miniature baked alaska was a special course I sent out after the dessert, it consisted of a flourless chocolate cake base topped with a scoop of ice cream, all encased in a fluffy meringue, torched tableside.

FLOURLESS CHOCOLATE CAKE

8g salt
165g butter
425g sugar
8 eggs
120g cocoa powder

Cream the sugar, butter, and salt together with a stand mixer using the paddle attachment. Add in the 8 eggs one by one, emulsifying each egg into the batter before adding the next. Add in the cocoa powder and mix thoroughly. Spread the batter out evenly onto a greased parchment-lined half sheet pan and bake at 350°F for 15 minutes. Once cooled, flip the cake upside down onto a new sheet of parchment then cut out 2 inch rounds. Reserve, layered with parchment paper, in an airtight container in the freezer.

MERINGUE

2 egg whites
50g sugar

Beat whites in a stand mixer on medium-high speed. When frothy, shear in sugar then beat until glossy and stiff peaks form.

PLATING

Place the round of cake in the center of the plate. Then add a scoop of the ice cream of your choice on top of the cake. Allow to freeze for 2 hours before covering the ice cream and cake with the meringue using an offset spatula. Reserve in the freezer until ready to be served. When ready, toast the meringue using a blowtorch and serve.

Mignardise

BONBON

Bonbons are pretty. That's why I put them on the menu. Need I say more? These things were probably the most annoying and finicky things to make, but also my favorite mignardise to eat.

BONBON SHELL

For 12 hemisphere bonbons:
90g 70% chocolate

Heat 60g of the chocolate to 57°C in a double boiler. Take the chocolate off the heat and add the remaining 30g chocolate and mix together. While stirring, cool the chocolate to 28°C. Put the chocolate back on the double boiler and bring back to 33°C. Use to case molds immediately or hold at temperature.

GUANAJA GANACHE

8g invert sugar
33g cream
33g 70% chocolate
5g butter

Melt the ingredients minus the butter together in a double boiler. When melted, bring off the heat and emulsify together. When the ganache cools to 35°C add the butter and emulsify again. Use to fill bonbon immediately or hold at temperature.

DULCEY GANACHE

25g cream
50g 32% chocolate
3g invert sugar
4g butter

Melt the ingredients minus the butter together in double boiler. When melted, bring off the heat and emulsify together. When the ganache cools to 35°C add the butter and emulsify again. Use to fill bonbon immediately or hold at temperature.

ASSEMBLY

Temper the colored cocoa butter to 30°C. Then brush the molds with the cocoa butter. Allow the cocoa butter to harden and set. Then fill each of the cavities in the mold with the tempered chocolate. Tap the molds to release any air bubbles. Turn the mold over and tap so that only a thin layer of chocolate remains in the cavity. Scrape the molds so that there is no more chocolate on the surface of the mold and allow to set and harden upside down so any residual chocolate does not pool at the bottom of the cavity. Fill the cavities with the ganache, leaving room for the final layer of chocolate. Tap the molds to level the ganache and allow to set. Top the ganache with more tempered chocolate before tapping again release any air bubbles. Level the bottoms with a bench scraper. Allow to fully set and harden. Make sure that the bonbons are fully released from the mold before overturning and demoulding.

CARAMEL

While I was staging at Chez TJ, the pastry chef there taught me how to hand wrap caramels with cellophane. Some of my favorite times working there was spent wrapping caramels, talking to the pastry chef about life and the restaurant industry. Being seventeen and in way over my head at the restaurant, I learned so much over those conversations of who I was and what I wanted to pursue.

CARAMEL

375g sugar
100g glucose
600g cream
4g salt
2.5g cream of tartar

Combine the ingredients in a large saucepan and cook on high heat for ~14 min, or until a light caramel color. Allow to cool and set in a greased loaf pan. Cut the caramels and wrap with cellophane sheets.

Note: Infuse the cream with tea for ~25 minutes or until fragrant to make tea-scented caramels. I recommend using either jasmine or oolong tea.

MADELEINE

Warm, freshly-baked madeleines are just about some of the tastiest things ever. I had never had a fresh madeleine until my time at The Plumed Horse where they served them as one of their mignardise. It was life-changing.

MINI MADELEINE

38g butter
5g dark brown sugar
5g honey
33g sugar
salt
40g all-purpose flour
1.3g baking powder
1 egg
fresh orange
candied orange

Melt the butter, dark brown sugar, and honey together in a pot. In a separate bowl, whisk together the sugar, pinch of salt, flour, baking powder, and egg. Whisk in the melted butter mixture. Add the zest of half an orange and stir together. Cover with cling film and let sit in fridge over-night. Transfer to a piping bag and pipe into a greased mini madeleine pan ⅔ way full before topping with pieces of the candied orange. Bake for 6-8 minutes in a 375°F oven. Immediately demold the madeleines by inverting the pan and tapping. Serve warm.

FORTUNE COOKIE

First originated in San Francisco, fortune cookies are probably the most Chinese-American treat of all time. The earl grey in the cookies are an ode to Dame Judi Dench and her British-ness. Folding these cookies was always a painful experience but having guests crack them open to find a note that said "THANK YOU FOR DINING AT DENCH." was always fun.

EARL GREY FORTUNE COOKIE

60g all-purpose flour
18g rice flour
2.5g cornstarch
1g salt
100g sugar
2 egg whites
34g neutral oil
23g water
1g vanilla extract

Whisk together the flour, rice flour, cornstarch, salt, and sugar in a bowl. In a separate bowl, whisk together the egg whites until frothy. Create a well in the middle of the dry ingredients. Pour the canola oil, water, and vanilla extract into the center of the well. Use a rubber spatula to stir in the wet ingredients. Stir until all the dry ingredients are well blended. Add half of the egg whites. Mix well to break up any lumps. When smooth, incorporate the remaining egg whites. Mix until smooth. Pipe or spoon the batter about the size of a quarter onto a silpat. Using the back of a spoon, spread the batter into a thin circle. Sprinkle earl grey tea leaves on the batter. Bake at 350°F for 10 minutes until slightly brown around the edges. Remove from oven and with an offset spatula, carefully and quickly scrape the fortune circles off the silpat and flip them over. Place a fortune strip in the center of the cookie. Immediately fold them in half then crease the middle of the cookie on the edge of a pan or a cup to shape. Place the folded fortune cookies into a muffin pan to cool. Store in an airtight container with silica desiccant packets.

MENDIANT

Mendiants are a traditional French treat eaten on the holidays. They consist of a disc of chocolate topped with exactly four different things. These things can be anything from dried fruits, to nuts, to pretty much anything you would want on a piece of chocolate.

CHOCOLATE MENDIANT

tempered chocolate
maldon sea salt
crunchy chocolate pearls
freeze dried fruit

Pipe the tempered chocolate into quarter-sized dots onto an acetate-lined sheet tray. Tap the tray on a flat surface to flatten the dots into discs. Top the discs with the sea salt, pearls, and freeze-dried fruits. Allow the chocolate to set and harden.

PAVLOVA

While scrolling through Francisco Migoya's *The Elements of Dessert*, I stumbled across a recipe that had a meringue with heavy cream powder incorporated into it so that the meringue had notes of dairy in it. I thought it would be interesting to do a version of pavlova: a dessert comprised of meringue, whipped cream, and berries. This mini pavlova consists of a dehydrated heavy cream meringue topped with freeze dried berries and a fresh mint leaf.

BERRY PAVLOVA

74g egg white
148g sugar
30g water
50g heavy cream powder
freeze dried strawberry
freeze dried raspberry
freeze dried blueberry
mint

Add the sugar and water into saucepan and bring to 240°F-250°F. Whip the egg whites until foamy in a stand mixer then pour in the sugar syrup slowly on medium speed, streaming the syrup onto the side of the bowl. Whip the meringue until stiff peaks form. Allow meringue to cool before folding in the heavy cream powder with a spatula. Pipe meringue into quarter-sized kisses on to silpat. Using a wet finger, press the tops of meringue inward to create a divot. Crush the freeze dried berries together then sprinkle on top of meringues. Dehydrate meringues in a 200°F oven for 2-2.5 hours or until fully dry and crunchy. Allow to cool and reserve in a airtight container with silica desiccant packets. When serving, top the pavlovas with a micro mint leaf.

ADDITIONAL RECIPES

BASIL POWDER

basil

Arrange basil leaves in a dehydrator set at 95°F. Let dehydrate for 24 hours or until dry. Blend leaves in a spice grinder until powdered.

OLIVE OIL POWDER

25g high quality extra virgin olive oil
tapioca maltodextrin

Add tapioca maltodextrin to the oil, a spoonful at a time, before massaging the maltodextrin into the oil with you hands. Continue to add the tapioca maltodextrin to the oil and massaging until a powder forms. The powder should dissolve immediately on your tongue. Reserve in an airtight container with silica desiccant packets.

COCONUT POWDER

25g unrefined coconut oil
tapioca maltodextrin

Melt the coconut oil until completely liquid. Allow to cool enough to be handled. Add tapioca maltodextrin to the oil, a spoonful at a time, before massaging the maltodextrin into the oil with you hands. Continue to add the tapioca maltodextrin to the oil and massaging until a powder forms. The powder should dissolve immediately on your tongue. Reserve in an airtight container with silica desiccant packets.

SORBET SYRUP

250g water
40g sugar
5g sorbet stabilizer
160g sugar
50g glucose powder

Marry sugar and sorbet stabilizer together in a container. Warm the water in a pot, then whisk in the sugar/stabilizer and bring to a boil. Add the rest of the sugar/glucose powder and boil 30 seconds. Allow to cool and let rest in fridge overnight.

MACERATED STRAWBERRY

20g small diced strawberries
3g sugar

Cover the strawberries with the sugar and allow to sit for at least 2 hours in the refrigerator.

STRAWBERRY MERINGUE

2 egg whites
50g sugar
freeze dried strawberry powder

Beat egg whites on medium-high speed. When frothy, shear the sugar in and beat until stiff peaks form. Using an offset spatula, spread the meringue thin on a silpat and dust strawberry powder over the top. Allow to dehydrate in oven set at 200°F for 2 hours or until dry and crisp. Let cool before breaking into shards, then store in an airtight container with silica desiccant packets until needed.

COCOA DUSTED MERINGUE

2 egg whites
50g sugar
cocoa powder

Beat egg whites on medium-high speed. When frothy, shear the sugar in and beat until stiff peaks form. Using a piping bag, pipe small meringue kisses onto a silpat. Dust cocoa powder over the tops of the meringues. Allow to dehydrate in oven set at 200°F for 2 hours or until dry and crisp. Let cool then store in an airtight container with silica desiccant packets until needed.

MERINGUE TUBES

2 egg whites
50g sugar

Beat egg whites on medium-high speed. When frothy, shear the sugar in and beat until stiff peaks form. Transfer to a piping bag and pipe tubes onto a silicone baking mat. Allow to dehydrate in oven set at 200°F for 2 hours or until dry and crisp. Let cool then store in an airtight container with silica desiccant packets until needed.

BASIL MERINGUE

2 egg whites
50g sugar
basil powder

Beat egg whites on medium-high speed. When frothy, shear the sugar in and beat until stiff peaks form. Using an offset spatula, spread the meringue thin on a silpat and dust basil powder over the top. Allow to dehydrate in oven set at 200°F for 2 hours or until dry and crisp. Let cool before breaking into shards, then store in an airtight container with silica desiccant packets until needed.

Timeline

& Layout

TIMELINE

THURSDAY

6:30 PM
pick up produce from the farmer's market

7:00 PM
grab a quick bite to eat

7:30 PM
go to other local markets to pick up the rest of the ingredients

8:30 PM
come home and juice fruits for sorbets, granita, foams, and gels and make ice cream bases

10:00 PM
finish clearing down and do some homework

1:00 AM
go to bed

FRIDAY

8:20 AM
wake up for class

12:00 PM
finish class and go pick up seafood

1:00 PM
eat lunch and take a quick nap

3:00 PM
begin egg dish prep

3:30 PM
start pastry prep by spinning ice creams and sorbets, making mousses, batters, panna cottas, crémeux, tuiles, meringues, shaping butter

6:45 PM
begin on mignardise by baking off fortune cookies and wrapping caramels

7:15 PM
eat something

7:30 PM
head to campus fellowship

10:30 PM
come home and finish making bonbons or other mignardises

12:30 AM
clear down and go to bed

TIMELINE

SATURDAY

10:30 AM
get out of bed, make bed, vacuum, mop, answer emails, do some work

2:00 PM
begin bread dough

2:30 PM
finish dessert prep by baking off batters, cutting mousses, ganaches, prepping fruits

3:30 PM
begin savory prep by peeling and bagging eggs, prepping vegetables and proteins

4:00 PM
shape bread dough

4:30 PM
eat a bagel

6:00 PM
bake off bread and begin prepping all garnishes

6:30 PM
arrange dining settings, finish all prep, tidy up kitchen

6:45 PM
queue up the DENCH. playlist, drop proteins in the water bath, do a final check on everything

7:00 PM
guests arrive and service begins

9:00 PM
guests leave and clear down begins

10:00 PM
finish washing dishes, hand dry silverware and glassware, take out the trash

10:30 PM
run out and grab dinner for myself

1:00 AM
go to bed

SUNDAY

8:20 AM
wake up and go to church

11:00 AM
grab lunch and take another nap

2:00 PM
hand dry rest of the dishware and completely reset, deep clean the kitchen

Check out the DENCH. playlist on Spotify:

DENCH.
POP-UP RESTAURANT
San Luis Obispo, CA

---

steamed pacific oyster
xo sauce – cilantro

hokkaido milk bread
cultured butter

62° tea egg
lapsang souchong – king trumpet –

pork tenderloin
bok choy –

FLOOR PLAN

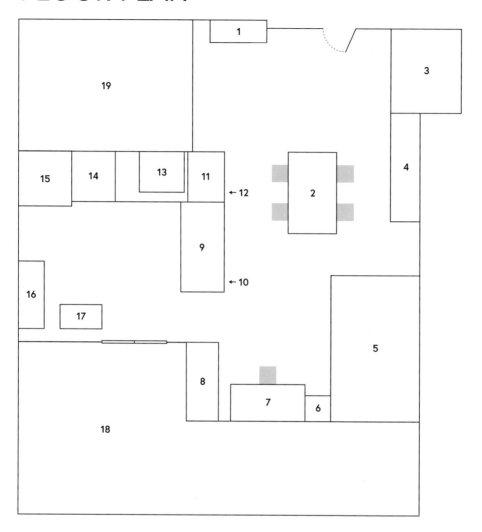

1 Shoe Rack	11 Drying Rack
2 Dining Table	12 *Under:* Dehydrator
3 Closet	13 Sink
4 Shelf	14 Stove
5 Bed	15 Fridge
6 Nightstand	16 Ingredients, Appliances, Deli Containers, Pot Storage
7 Desk	17 Towel Storage, Rolling Shelf
8 Mixing Bowls, Appliances, Pantry, Small Tools, Plateware, Dry Ingredients, Baking Sheet Pans	18 Outdoor Balcony
9 Prep Table	19 Bathroom
10 *Under:* Chamber Vacuum Sealer, Small Tools Small Appliances, Stand Mixer, Blowtorch	

"I never knew a luh, luh-luh love like this

Gotta be somethin' for me to write this

...

As my reflection in light I'mma lead you

And whatever's right, I'mma feed you"

Common

ABOUT THE AUTHOR

JIMMY WONG is a fourth-year Food Science major at the California Polytechnic State University, San Luis Obispo. In his third year in school, Jimmy started the pop-up restaurant, DENCH., out of his studio apartment where he served a seven-course tasting menu for four people once a week where diners would enjoy their meals just a couple feet away from his bed.

For his senior project, Jimmy wrote this cookbook to document his experiences and recipes from the pop-up. Follow his work @jwongdynasty or on his website: www.denchrestaurant.com.